BLUE HUNGER

poems by

Terry Wolverton

Finishing Line Press
Georgetown, Kentucky

BLUE HUNGER

Copyright © 2018 by Terry Wolverton
ISBN 978-1-63534-754-8 First Edition
All rights reserved under International and Pan-American Copyright Conventions. No part of this book may be reproduced in any manner whatsoever without written permission from the publisher, except in the case of brief quotations embodied in critical articles and reviews.

ACKNOWLEDGMENTS

These poems were previously published:

"Burning History" and "Ceremonial Ghazal" ~ *Prairie Schooner*
"Ganges Petals" and "Song" ~ *Adrienne*
"Ghost Soup" ~ *Rock and Sling*
"Hyssie Fit" ~ *Gertrude*
"Kali Keeps It Real" and "Transient" ~ *Van Gogh's Ear*
"Off Vine" and "Thirteen Seasons: Haiku for Los Angeles" ~ *Cultural Weekly*
"Orifice" ~ *Poets Market*
"Paradelle in Response to the Question: How Would You Like to be Remembered" and "Too Long" ~ *Cream City Review*
"Theory of Everything" ~ *poetryrepairs.com*
"The Sum of Everything" ~ *Big City Lit, bigcitylit.com.*
"Tinnitus Lullaby" ~ *The River Muse, a Journal of Poetry and Art*
"Tundra," ~ *The Nervous Breakdown, www.thenervousbreakdown.com*
"Twisted Twister Twist" ~ *EVENT: a Trans-Genre Anthology, Viz. Inter-Arts*
"Untied" ~ *poeticdiversity.com*

Publisher: Leah Maines
Editor: Christen Kincaid
Cover Art: Yvonne M. Estrada
Author Photo: Yvonne M. Estrada
Cover Design: Terry Wolverton

Printed in the USA on acid-free paper.
Order online: www.finishinglinepress.com
also available on amazon.com

Author inquiries and mail orders:
Finishing Line Press
P. O. Box 1626
Georgetown, Kentucky 40324
U. S. A.

Table of Contents

Blue Hunger 1

i. "People think I'm tough but they don't see the wet wound"
Tundra 4
Too Long 5
Transient 6
Orifice 7
Roll 8
Hyssie Fit 9
The Sum of Everything 10
Tinnitus Lullaby 11
Rooster 12
Ghost Soup 13
Ceremonial Ghazal 14
Untied 15

ii. "yoked to a blue globe's hunger."
Twisted Twister Twist 18
Theory of Everything 19
Burning History 21
New Museums 23
Song 24
Off Vine 25
Thirteen Seasons: Haiku for Los Angeles 26

iii. "Let us dance, my love, tango 'til our dark worlds unravel."
Long Night Moon 30
Kali Keeps It Real 31
Ganges Petals 32
Paradelle in Response to the Question, "How Would
    You Like to Be Remembered?" 33

BLUE HUNGER

That early mantra of the world
mantra of most ambition and tattered hunger,
mantra of blue smoke and seasoned regret,
broth of tears and ceremony,
dark fruit and coral cloud,
phrases yoked on a tiny necklace.

As if reaching for a tattered necklace,
fistful of poems to pour into the world,
face closed to the surrounding cloud,
set of the jaw cries hunger.
Once your eyes enter the dark ceremony,
the body learns not to reach toward regret.

This snake has moved in petals of regret,
shed its skirt of wonder like a necklace,
sweated through the smoky ceremony,
wearing the aroma of another world.
Elsewhere notice the immediate hunger,
sky opened to sun, then closed by cloud.

Sun reminds me of the fruit of clouds;
bitterness cooks a fistful of regret,
yoked to a blue globe's hunger.
Poems clustered on a jeweled necklace
until your shoes move into another world,
enter the invention of body ceremony.

Notice even the table glowed in ceremony.
Notice the unyielding bed of clouds.
Notice the first day of the world.
Notice the moist body of regret.
Hope for the return of memory's necklace,
flavors emanating from the stew of hunger.

You learned to reach for broth of hunger,
return and return to ceremony,
wear wonder like a globe necklace,
cluster phrases into clouds.
Have you learned not to keep regret,
but shed it like the petals of the world?

Enter the world with blue hunger.
Open to mantra of ceremony and regret.
Wear necklace of roses, skirt of clouds.

i.

"*People think I'm tough
but they don't see the wet wound*"

TUNDRA

Tundra, come in from the cold. Sit down
by firelight of this last world and thaw
your aching bones. If you remember
any stories, tell them now, before
the room dissolves and flows into sea.

Oceans overwhelm their shores and land
is all awash. Soon evolution
will run backward; we'll be aquatic
once more. Tundra, you're a pretty word
printed in waterlogged books. Tundra,

you're the name of my unborn daughter.
You're a faint lullaby I whisper
in my lover's ear at night. Tundra,
you're the straw harp I play in heaven.
Lay your frigid cheek against my lap;

let me strum you to sleep. Your strings
slice the tips of my fingers; speckles
of ice sprinkle out, glint on crimson
cloth. This is how I know you've entered
my heart, Tundra, with your frosted light.

TOO LONG

Too long I've been trapped in the false polarity of mother and armed robbery
Eggs sizzle on the skillet while I dance tango
and lies spill from my mouth like shiny coins

I don't care much for guns but they look good in a woman's hand
I don't care much for babies
Eggs are about all I can tolerate but even then I shatter their fragile skulls

People think I'm tough but they don't see the wet wound
My own mother married her bitterness and stayed faithful
Our globe is crowded with lapsed fathers

We are sentenced for our crimes of need, of innocence
The smell of gasoline is everywhere
its dark music overwhelms the weeping

I take my eggs scrambled with a side of ammunition
Tango enacts the polarity of nomads
Are we not all babies in our grasping?

TRANSIENT

I've been driving for hours past nothing.
I wonder if I've died and just don't know.
Not even birds disrupt the white sky;
no radio signals for miles.

I wonder if I've died and just don't know,
my fingers stiffened on the steering wheel.
No radio signal for miles;
to what music do the dead listen?

Fingers stiffened on the steering wheel,
I keep veering over the double yellow line.
To what music do the dead listen?
I have only old songs to sing.

I keep veering over the double yellow line;
at what point will I fall off the edge?
I have only old songs to sing,
songs of Jesus, songs of Indian maids.

At what point did I fall off the edge?
Faster I go, more the horizon recedes.
Songs of Jesus, songs of Indian maids
embedded in the whine of the tires.

Faster I go, more the horizon recedes.
Odometer rolls to a line of zeroes.
Embedded in the whine of the tires,
the lonesome echo of the world.

Odometer rolls to a line of zeroes;
not even birds disrupt the white sky.
Lonesome echoes through the world.
I've been driving for hours past nothing.

ORIFICE

Mothers disappear
in a forgotten language,
follow distraction,
a war of bright chords
flood of tin vowels.

We tongue the endings,
become the memory,
fly blind toward some
lost source, clumsy
with caution and faith.

It's a long shot, but
we're not circumspect;
we follow the light and heat
of our small hunches, burning
toward the long sound of her.

ROLL

Like Saint Francis, my grandmother had her entourage.
All-girl band, they followed her like an eruption,

Menstrual birds, veins like candy,
purse pulse and apple lipstick.

Cousins under the skin,
they snacked on Bandaids and aspirin.

Snapshot from the road: coins and
cracked fountain. The wrecked compass.

She visits a mistaken room in a complex town,
women sipping plasma milkshakes at the hotel bar,

a jarring stop on the body highway.
She buys a familiar souvenir of death:

Another dictionary strewn with secrets
a map detouring into herky-jerky worlds.

HYSSIE FIT

Numbers are everyday milestones,
a finger in chalk, the wreckage of
consciousness, everything born
will die—is this not the vision we
recreate, blackboard in shards, formulae
shattered into years, hysteria
just another potential sine,
an abstract theory of female
tendencies, mathematical frame for
defining a womb emotional,
my natural organs shocking and
wrong, that's the message they intend me
to find at the drive-thru lobotomy
hut, where I've washed myself clean of those
in-born limitations and scattered
my once-perfect cloth in the dead dust.

THE SUM OF EVERYTHING

Maybe sleep is half-remembered travel,
a bicycle upside down in the wreckage
of someone's discarded day. Flowers
inhabit the world of senses, loose
and empty their identities—yellow
and white—in the suspension of landscape,
streets and rooms expanding like paper
petals, forgetting their unfamiliar moons.

You are in my pocket, a transformed light.
The context is left to those who know
what words mean, those reflected nightmares,
liminal dreams. Memory can enter,
suck the day of colors, its nectared heat.
Now can seem stretched far into another
definition, collaged with eyes and trees
and purple stems. Enter; all awaits you.

Someone knows the sum of everything.
Death's scrutiny erases the happened,
hectic intrusion of ideas.
We may leave knowing little of this flaming
life, only the bright yellow pollen
glowing like sun on the half-remembered sheet.
Dress me in your particular found song
and hold me, shake my willing white petals.

TINNITUS LULLABY

Is the night swollen with birdsong
or are my cochleae singing
to me again, phantom echo
of sounds I once heard in pre-dawn
India, when trees came alive?

I called you across continents
so you too could hear the music
of birds awakening beside
the temple that glowed like a lantern,
while sacred chants poured from windows,
rippling across dark water.

I've always been lonely. The world
leaves its fingerprints on me,
but all I touch dissolves to smoke,
and I'm left listening only
to the music inside my head.

ROOSTER

You've been someone else too long.
You've come to identify with her
blonde wig, stained fingernails, tiara.
We've grown accustomed to your little
monologues, heavy with death slang.

You've forgotten how to converse with rocks;
you hate their inertness, their fixity.
Smoke blooms from the end of your constant
cigarette; the ash grows longer, drops.
The acid day pierces your illusions.

Ideas are cooked slow in a calm eye.
The nipple is smarter than the brain.
You fail to perceive the other versions
of your story. Backyard rooster left,
can no longer show where the treasure hides.

If you could re-wind the scene, would you?
Now you sit in a room. Rock and want.
After death we no longer worry
cigarette dreams of the monkey brain
or recognize the sound of feathers.

GHOST SOUP

Woman in the nursing home says, "I don't know why I'm here. I'm already dead."

Cempasúchil fragrant on altars for the dead.

Hungry ghosts who yearn for what they cannot swallow.

I've told you truths that once I could not stomach.

Andrew facebooks: "Tell me a secret. Or give me praise."

The photo of us in which your smile is easy, your eyes luminous.

The partial carcass of the baby rat left on the driveway by the white cat.

Elaine facebooks: "Pray for my mother who died yesterday." Chant to release her soul.

The year is turning whether we like it or not. Each day there is less light.

You text: "I've known and loved you for 100,000 lives."

Water in the reservoir today like dark glass on which ducks glide.

Dear heart, when my mood turns, it's just a ghost walking through me

on its way to somewhere else.

CEREMONIAL GHAZAL

Drape my igneous hips in a girdle of bone
strung gleanings from charnel field's clutter of bone

You dwell in a country of exile and hush
each night I cross over that border of bone

I sought sleep's relief in your stonemason's arms
lull me to dream in a cradle of bone

Twenty year's journey on sheet metal sea
steering my ship with a paddle of bone

My broken throat cries for a sheltering sip
pour me a cup from your ladle of bone

Knit vision to language, braid words into blood
weave daylight to dark with a shuttle of bone

Live in your skeleton, lodge in your skin
build your strong house with a girder of bone.

UNTIED

After the accident, my body was
no longer a flower. I noticed your
eyes turn from my Tumeric skin, mouth spilled
over a vacant face. An exposed ache.
There was no remedy for that mirror,
reluctance of your fingertips to claim
me, not quite smile eluding my naked
light. I began to believe my bloodstream
was radioactive, that my womb glowed
strange and bright. Nothing could keep us safe, not
ritual or remembrance, not laughter
or one still breath. This deeper knowledge poured
through the days until our minds could hold it,
body cleansed of its meaning, need untied.

ii.

"yoked to a blue globe's hunger."

TWISTED TWISTER TWIST

Tempests wheel, incite sepulchral trees, electrocute daylight. Thwart with impalpable sabotage. Threaten escapist reticence. Temptress waves. Indolent souls try to wallow in sacred trysts. Epitaphs raw, tersely written. Ingratitude seethes, triumphant testicles wither. Ink spills tantalize every demon. Thunder waits impassively, sucks tearful elation. Remember, thoughts withheld invoke strange testimony. Even Darwin trembled when intimate silence tangled. Ever resourceful, twilight waltzes in sonorous time; evening devolves toward wretched intoxication. Suppose touch. Triage wanton insurrections, suppress truth. Elegant death transforms wicked indifference, seizes tomorrow's emergent reverence. Temporary windows inhale sedative tropes, elide reflection. Torture whispers insistent song, tiptoes trancelike while it savors tea. Elliptical dharma. Twisted wistful ictus, strictest trickster.

THEORY OF EVERYTHING

> *In theoretical physics, M-theory is an extension of string theory in which 11 dimensions are identified.* —Wikipedia

A string walks into a bar
Cool light sidles her sheer length
The jukebox plays "Fly Me to the Moon"

A string walks into a bar
The jukebox plays "Come Fly with Me"
In the corner booth, a rusty knife

A string walks into a bar
In the corner booth, a blunt knife
nurses a Pabst Blue Ribbon

A string walks into a bar
orders a Pabst Blue Ribbon
swivels onto a tall stool

A string walks into a bar
slides onto a vacant stool
awaits the bartender's benediction

A string walks into a bar
receives a tall, cool benediction
She looks around for a light

A string walks into a bar
scrounges her purse for a light
The bowl of bar nuts is down to a snowdrift of salt

A string walks into a bar
Salt from the bar nuts sucks moisture from her tongue
She traces initials carved into the wooden ledge

A string walks into a bar
She traces initials that might once have been hers
her eyes fill at the memory

A string walks into a bar
Memory spontaneously combusts
Ice dies in the bottom of a glass

A string walks into a bar
Ice cracks open as it melts
Blue neon shadows her sheer length.

BURNING HISTORY

Half a world away, ashes
from the gutted library sift through empty
streets, deserted even by soldiers
whose weapons aimed to waste
a regime, not spare a civilization.
Smoke filters the sun white.

California poet, I finger my white
page, try to coax words from the ashes
of my overburdened brain. Civilization
keeps speeding up, gobbling the empty
spaces in the calendar. Is poetry a waste
of time, pursuit of fools, not soldiers?

I'd never don the uniform of soldier.
I'd rather dress in layers of white,
take my begging bowl, waste
my education, than to smart bomb to ashes
this old city. It would hollow me, empty
me to ravage an ancient civilization.

And what could we mean when we say "civilization"
if our conflicts are still settled by soldiers?
All night I sing to the empty
moon, her arms so cold and white.
I rub my eyes to flush the ashes
out; on my hands, the stench of waste.

I used to spend my days wasted,
having turned my back on civilization,
recycling the ashes
from my pipe, convinced of my superiority to soldiers.
I had the luck of being white:
I could choose to keep my mind empty.

But now I feel the world more empty
for the loss of books I never read. History wasted,
pages once bone white
now cinder; what will be lost to civilization?
I find myself believing that the soldiers
could have saved the library, but let it burn to ashes.

These words are ashes on an empty
afternoon. Words are not soldiers. Wasted
civilizations return to essence, white.

NEW MUSEUMS

The museum of today is littered
with burned carcasses; legs, arms erupt in
all directions. Couch potatoes pretend
to look, but their eyes are occupied with
the same blank stares, brains not agitated
by each new attack. The guard remembers
his ragged prayers, howls his flat-voiced song.

The museum of tomorrow contains
a tree, stone remnant of something that grew,
in a neighborhood, maybe, a backyard.
It contains morning and afternoon. Night
was stolen by some motherfucker that
was not caught. The guard is fascinated
by the hole it leaves in his brain and heart.

SONG

All the songs sing about man problems
precious night stolen, she goes unchosen
rubbing bloodshot the hard ring on her finger
he, a thief of sonnets, her blouse dancing vulgar
her youth dangling from a torch gone cold

Songs in an older voice, more faceted
words born carved, precisely guarded
more skin and whiskey, more harsh surfaces
a ragged perimeter, she sings of
the girl she was before the granite poem

Old music, tuneless and rotten, clustered
its stories bulging with teeth and stone
her eyes obsidian when she calls upon
a bolder self, glittering and mad and rare
words refusing the lesser relief of time.

OFF VINE

Its attic burned clear through
a blackened shell
atop that yellow house
where only weeks before
I'd dined with Kim,
just recently returned to writing poetry.

Her eyes sparked over the wine,
cantos crackled from her lips.
I could hear the sizzle of her skin
as something re-ignited in her,
some fuel blazing for herself
after years of shining light on others.

"I can't stop," she told me,
"The words erupt like fever;
I can't stop singing to the page.
It's all I want to do all day.
Makes me want to neglect my clients,
forget a life bound in tidy paragraphs."

Now the walls that witnessed us
are scorched, crumbling; the table
where we sat splintered; wineglass
shattered; tablecloth is ash.
Kim is writing poetry
and the sirens echo the night long.

THIRTEEN SEASONS: HAIKUS FOR LOS ANGELES

For Andrew

1. Winter
We don't know how to
drive in rain, gaze boggled by
glow of green green hills.

2. Eighty Degrees of Winter
Poppies awaken
early from their naps; flip-flops
in February.

3. Oscar night
Red carpet blankets
the whole city. Fame, like fire,
makes its own weather.

4. Signs of spring
At the reservoir
herons return to nest in
eucalyptus trees.

5. Allergy season
Pollens spiral through
engorged cavities. I snort
spring like an addict.

6. Jacaranda season
Purpled, petaled skies
unhinge the mind. Miracles
come and go so fast.

7. June Gloom
Fog descends on June;
each morning stalled, bubble-wrapped
till late afternoon.

8. Summer
Marine haze lingers,
never quite burns off; white sun
veiled behind white sky.

9. Smog season
Wherever I look
is brown—hills, sky. Why trust air
if you can't see it?

10. Late Summer
Twilight comes early,
amber hour of day, palm trees
dark against gold sky

11. Santa Anas
Desert comes to town
on the hot breath of winds. Palm
leaves crack, fly, crash down.

12. Burn Season
Fire leaps the freeway.
Ash dusts the windshield, sunsets
rage purple and orange.

13. Holiday Season
The white cat comes in
at night now, curls close to your
sleeping, flannelled form.

iii.

"*Let us dance, my love,
tango 'til our dark worlds unravel.*"

LONG NIGHT MOON

Seems so far away, her cold eye
high above. Surely she sees this churning world,
how we choke on money, hold
it more precious than water, than earth,
than air we can't breathe.
Surely she sees our hands up,
sees the scorched ghosts of students
rising from the riverbed,
a jungle of missing girls,
and young women dragging their blood
soaked mattresses through the streets.

A friend of mine, a yogi, vows
to speak no criticism or complaint
for 40 days. Does she turn her eyes
inward? Does she swallow her rage?
Or does the silence cleanse her mind?
Purify her dream of a different world?
The pearled Moon is silent too,
a beacon in this long night.

KALI KEEPS IT REAL

My teeth leave bruises on your shoulders, but I don't draw blood.
Not from you, love. Unless you leave. Then I'll swill your raw blood.

Vermillion mother of your unremembered nightmares.
You scrabbled to open your stuck-shut eyes; still you saw blood.

When I bite, red swamps my throat, evicts words grown meaningless.
Bright with plasma, more real than language in my craw—blood.

Am I not beautiful, in my necklace of strung skulls?
Unsmiling, blank-eyed and bleached as they are of the jaw blood.

I have four arms; still I cannot hold you. Instead wield swords
to slice through love's ripe illusion, lay bare your straw blood.

Let us dance, my love, tango 'til our dark worlds unravel.
Let us writhe in burning battle, hot enough to thaw blood.

It's my third eye that scans the future. Kali devours Time.
Years swirl past my barbed fingertips, leave only this scrawled blood.

GANGES PETALS

You'd been curled around the flower of twin
doubts: the potato sack race from the womb
and the wistful boat on fire, its cargo
of ash. You were a poem caught in body
absence, a shape consumed by light. Water
played its own inexplicable ballad,
extolling shadow and time. Waking, you
found painful, especially before
a day in flames, as if the hard hours
might strike your name. Instead you slept through most
of the mourner's song, faded vessel with
significant moments of love. Mantra
of an aging river carries habits
of loss. Your eyes never saw the scorched sea.

PARADELLE IN RESPONSE TO THE QUESTION, "HOW WOULD YOU LIKE TO BE REMEMBERED?"

When I am dead, cut up my poems; let each word fly
When I am dead, cut up my poems; let each word fly
Ashes in wind, sell my dresses in the streets of Paris
Ashes in wind, sell my dresses in the streets of Paris
I am my poems. Sell each in Paris, cut the word when.
Wind up dead on streets of ashes. Let my dresses fly.

Let ragpickers pilfer the best morsels
Let ragpickers pilfer the best morsels
and magpies pluck jewels from my throat
and magpies pluck jewels from my throat
Best the ragpickers' and magpies' pluck
Pilfer jewels let from my throat morsels.

When I am dead, forget my song. Bleach it of bitterness
When I am dead, forget my song. Bleach it of bitterness
Pledge yourself instead to other music
Pledge yourself instead to other music
When am yourself, bleach it to music instead.
I pledge my song of bitterness. Other dead forget.

Let Paris bleach yourself from my song.
When my dead dresses pilfer wind, magpies fly in streets
My best poems forget each other and my jewels cut.
When the dead pledge to sell morsels of bitterness
instead of music; pluck it. Let up.
I am ashes in ragpicker's throat. I am the word.

Terry Wolverton is the author of eleven books, including *Ruin Porn*, poetry; *Embers*, a novel in poems; and *Insurgent Muse: life and art at the Woman's Building*, a memoir. She is the founder of Writers At Work, a creative writing studio in Los Angeles, and Affiliate Faculty in the MFA Writing Program at Antioch University Los Angeles. She is also an instructor of Kundalini Yoga and Meditation. www.terrywolverton.com.

www.ingramcontent.com/pod-product-compliance
Lightning Source LLC
LaVergne TN
LVHW041600070426
835507LV00011B/1201